CAMBRIDGE PRIMARY
Science

Skills Builder

3

Jon Board and Alan Cross

CAMBRIDGE
UNIVERSITY PRESS

University Printing House, Cambridge CB2 8BS, United Kingdom

One Liberty Plaza, 20th Floor, New York, NY 10006, USA

477 Williamstown Road, Port Melbourne, VIC 3207, Australia

314–321, 3rd Floor, Plot 3, Splendor Forum, Jasola District Centre, New Delhi – 110025, India

79 Anson Road, #06–04/06, Singapore 079906

Cambridge University Press is part of the University of Cambridge.

It furthers the University's mission by disseminating knowledge in the pursuit of education, learning and research at the highest international levels of excellence.

www.cambridge.org
Information on this title: www.cambridge.org/9781316611029

© Cambridge University Press 2016

This publication is in copyright. Subject to statutory exception and to the provisions of relevant collective licensing agreements, no reproduction of any part may take place without the written permission of Cambridge University Press.

First published 2016

20 19 18 17 16 15 14 13 12 11 10

Produced for Cambridge University Press by
White-Thomson Publishing
www.wtpub.co.uk

Editor: Rachel Minay
Designer: Clare Nicholas

Printed in Great Britain by Ashford Colour Press Ltd.

A catalogue record for this publication is available from the British Library

ISBN 978-1-316-61102-9 Paperback

Cambridge University Press has no responsibility for the persistence or accuracy of URLs for external or third-party internet websites referred to in this publication, and does not guarantee that any content on such websites is, or will remain, accurate or appropriate. Information regarding prices, travel timetables, and other factual information given in this work is correct at the time of first printing but Cambridge University Press does not guarantee the accuracy of such information thereafter.

Cover artwork: Bill Bolton

....

NOTICE TO TEACHERS IN THE UK
It is illegal to reproduce any part of this work in material form (including photocopying and electronic storage) except under the following circumstances:
(i) where you are abiding by a licence granted to your school or institution by the Copyright Licensing Agency;
(ii) where no such licence exists, or where you wish to exceed the terms of a licence, and you have gained the written permission of Cambridge University Press;
(iii) where you are allowed to reproduce without permission under the provisions of Chapter 3 of the Copyright, Designs and Patents Act 1988, which covers, for example, the reproduction of short passages within certain types of educational anthology and reproduction for the purposes of setting examination questions.

Contents

Introduction	4
1 Looking after plants	**5**
1.1 Plants and their parts	6
1.2 Plants need light and water	8
1.3 Transporting water	10
1.4 Plant growth and temperature	12
2 Looking after ourselves	**13**
2.1 Food groups	14
2.2 A healthy diet	16
2.3 An unhealthy diet	17
2.4 Exercise and sleep	19
3 Living things	**21**
3.1 Living and non-living	22
3.2 Growth and nutrition	24
3.3 Movement and reproduction	26
3.4 Sorting humans	28
3.5 Sorting living things	29
4 Our five senses	**31**
4.1 Hearing and touch	32
4.2 Taste and smell	33
4.3 Sight	35
5 Investigating materials	**36**
5.1 Properties of materials	37
5.2 Sorting materials	38
5.5 Magnetic materials	40
6 Forces and movement	**41**
6.1 Push and pull	42
6.2 Changing shape	44
6.3 How big is that force?	46
6.4 Forcemeters	47
6.5 Friction	50
Answers	**52**
Glossary	**57**

Introduction

This series of primary science activity books complements *Cambridge Primary Science* and promotes, through practice, learner confidence and depth of knowledge in the skills of scientific enquiry (SE) and key scientific vocabulary and concepts. These activity books will:

- enhance and extend learners' scientific knowledge and facts
- promote scientific enquiry skills and learning in order to think like a scientist
- advance each learner's knowledge and use of scientific vocabulary and concepts in their correct context.

The *Skills Builder* activity books consolidate core topics that learners have *already* covered in the classroom, providing those learners with that extra reinforcement of SE skills, vocabulary topic knowledge and understanding. They have been written with a focus on scientific literacy with ESL/EAL learners in mind.

How to use the activity books

These activity books have been designed for use by individual learners, either in the classroom or at home. As teachers and as parents, you can decide how and when they are used by your learner to best improve their progress. The *Skills Builder* activity books target specific topics (lessons) from Grades 1–6 from all the units covered in *Cambridge Primary Science*. This targeted approach has been carefully designed to consolidate topics where help is most needed.

How to use the units

Unit introduction

Each unit starts with an introduction for you as the teacher or parent. It clearly sets out which topics are covered in the unit and the learning objectives of the activities in each section. This is where you can work with learners to select all, most or just one of the sections according to individual needs.

The introduction also provides advice and tips on how best to support the learner in the skills of scientific enquiry and in the practice of key scientific vocabulary.

Sections

Each section matches a corresponding lesson in the main series. Sections contain write-in activities that are supported by:

- Key words – key vocabulary for the topic, also highlighted in bold in the sections
- Key facts – a short fact to support the activities where relevant
- Look and learn – where needed, activities are supported with scientific exemplars for extra support of how to treat a concept or scientific method
- Remember – tips for the learner to steer them in the right direction.

How to approach the write-in activities

Teachers and parents are advised to provide students with a blank A5 notebook at the start of each grade for learners to use alongside these activity books. Most activities will provide enough space for the answers required. However, some learner responses – especially to enquiry-type questions – may require more space for notes. Keeping notes and plans models how scientists work and encourages learners to explore and record their thinking, leaving the activity books for the final, more focused answers.

Think about it questions

Each unit also contains some questions for discussion at home with parents, or at school. Although learners will record the outcomes of their discussions in the activity book, these questions are intended to encourage the students to think more deeply.

Self-assessment

Each section in the unit ends with a self-assessment opportunity for learners: empty circles with short learning statements. Teachers or parents can ask learners to complete the circles in a number of ways, depending on their age and preference, e.g. with faces, traffic light colours or numbers. The completed self-assessments provide teachers with a clearer understanding of how best to progress and support individual learners.

Glossary of key words and concepts

At the end of each activity book there is a glossary of key scientific words and concepts arranged by unit. Learners are regularly reminded to practise saying these words out loud and in sentences to improve communication skills in scientific literacy.

1 Looking after plants

What learners will practise and reinforce

The activities in this Skills Builder unit give learners further practice in the following topics in the Learner's Book and Activity Book:

Topic	In this topic, learners will:
1.1 Plants and their parts	name the four main parts of plants
1.2 Plants need light and water	learn that plants need light and water
1.3 Transporting water	investigate what happens to a plant without roots
1.4 Plant growth and temperature	learn that plants need warmth

Help your learner

In this unit, learners will practise observing and comparing objects, living things and events (Section 1.1). They will also draw conclusions from results and begin to use scientific knowledge to suggest explanations (Section 1.2). To help them:

1 Encourage learners to observe plants carefully. Ask them if they can see similarities or differences between plants, for example in the shape of their leaves.

2 Help learners to look in the local area for more evidence about how different plants grow in different conditions.

TEACHING TIP

Help learners to develop respect for their environment by looking after plants and handling them with care.

1.1 Plants and their parts

plant, leaves, stem, roots, flowers, soil

Plant parts

Use the key words to finish the labels on this **plant**.

Remember:
Say the key words out loud when you write them. It will help you remember them.

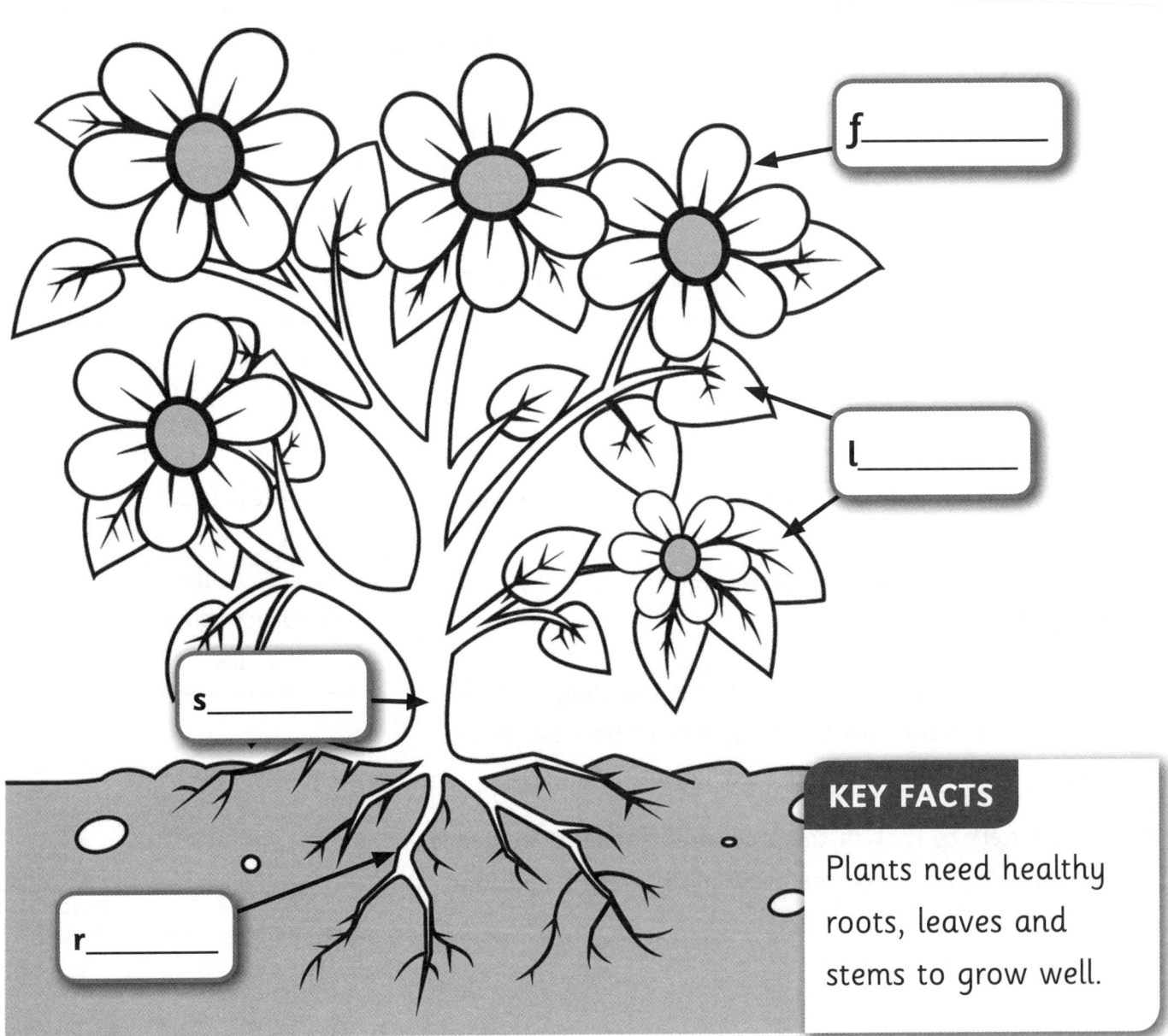

f_____

l_____

s_____

r_____

KEY FACTS

Plants need healthy roots, leaves and stems to grow well.

Label a real plant

Resources
You will need a real plant with flowers, some thin card, sticky tape and scissors.

1. Make labels for the parts of the plant using thin card.
2. Use sticky tape to stick each label on the plant.
3. Put a label for the roots into the **soil**.

CHECK YOUR LEARNING

◯ I can name the roots, stem, leaves and flowers of a plant.

1 Looking after plants 7

1.2 Plants need light and water

question, light, water, investigation, results, height, grow

Plant height

Luis has a **question**.

He does an **investigation** to find out.

These are the **results** after ten days.

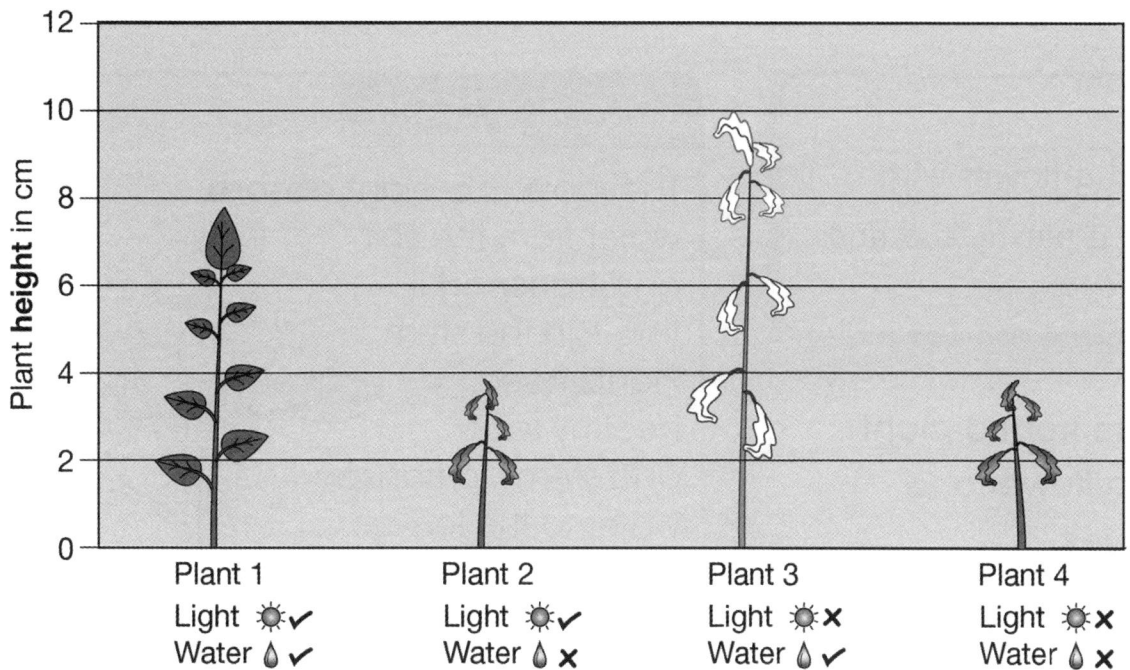

1. How many centimetres tall are the plants now?

   Plant 1 _____ Plant 2 _____ Plant 3 _____ Plant 4 _____

2. What does Plant 3 need to make it healthy?

   _____

3. What two things do plants need to **grow** well?

   _____ and _____

4. **Think about it!**

   Where do outdoor plants get water from?

   _____

CHECK YOUR LEARNING

○ I know that plants need light and water.

1.3 Transporting water

absorb, transport, predict

No roots!

Resources
You will need a flower with some leaves, a plastic cup and some soil.

LOOK AND LEARN
The roots of a plant **absorb** water from the soil and **transport** it through the stem. Plants need healthy roots and stems to transport water to the leaves.

water

1. Cut a stem from a plant that has a flower and some leaves.

2. Plant the stem in the soil in the plastic cup. You now have a plant with no roots.

3. Give your plant with no roots a little water every day.

4. **Predict** what you think will happen after one week and after two weeks.

Prediction

What will happen to the plant?	
After one week?	After two weeks?

10 1.3 Transporting water

5 Draw what the plant looked like after one week and after two weeks.

Results

What happened to the plant?	
After one week?	After two weeks?

6 Were your predictions correct? _____

Think about it!

7 Why do plants need healthy roots and stems?

_____

8 Explain what happened to the plant with no roots.

_____

CHECK YOUR LEARNING

◯ I know that roots absorb water from soil.

◯ I know that plants need healthy roots and stems to grow well.

1 Looking after plants **11**

1.4 Plant growth and temperature

temperature, thermometer, hot, warm, cold

What is the temperature?

1 Fill in the labels for each picture.

2 Think about it!

What would you do to help Plant 3 grow?

_____

CHECK YOUR LEARNING

◯ I know that plants can be too hot or too cold.

2 Looking after ourselves

What learners will practise and reinforce

The activities in this Skills Builder unit give learners further practice in the following topics in the Learner's Book and Activity Book:

Topic	In this topic, learners will:
2.1 Food groups	practise naming the five food groups practise which food goes in which group
2.2 A healthy diet	know which foods are healthy
2.3 An unhealthy diet	know why fat and sugar are unhealthy
2.4 Exercise and sleep	know why exercise is good for us

Help your learner

In this unit, learners will practise observing and comparing objects (Section 2.1) and making predictions and communicating these (Section 2.4). To help them:

1 Help your learner to practise organising food into food groups. Learners could do this at home by helping to plan healthy meals and getting involved in shopping and cooking.

2 Encourage learners at home to use simple equipment to weigh food items or measure volumes of liquids.

TEACHING TIP

Talk about what learners already know about a healthy diet and the other things that we need to stay healthy. This will help you decide which key concepts to practise in this unit.

2.1 Food groups

food group, carbohydrate, fruit and vegetables, dairy, protein, fat and sugar, unhealthy

Which food, which group?

Use the key words to label each **food group**.

Remember:
Practise identifying food groups at meals. This will increase your confidence and knowledge.

f_____ and s_____

c_____

p_____

f_____ and v_____

d_____

Food hunt

1 Look for some food or pictures of food. Say the name of the group the food is in. Can you find two foods from each group?

2 Write what you find in the table.

Food	Food group
rice	carbohydrate

3 Think about it!

Which food group do you think looks **unhealthy**?

CHECK YOUR LEARNING

◯ I can name the five food groups.

◯ I can say which food goes into which group.

2 Looking after ourselves

2.2 A healthy diet

diet, healthy

Healthy food I love

Remember:
Fruit and vegetables keep us healthy.

LOOK AND LEARN

Your **diet** is the food you eat. This food triangle shows a **healthy** diet.

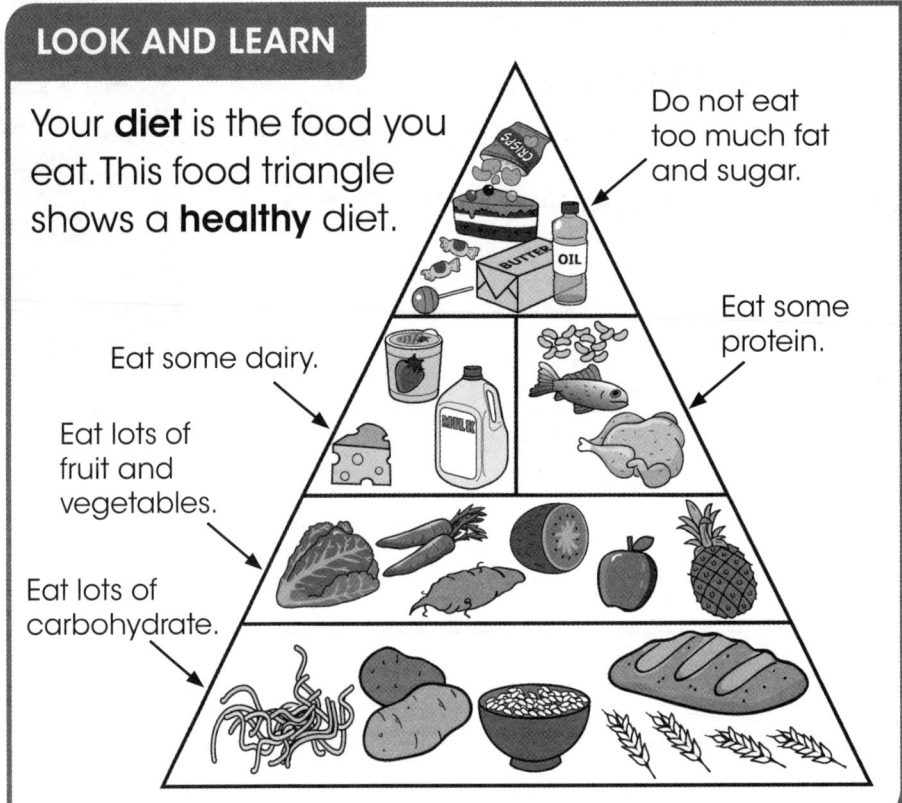

Do not eat too much fat and sugar.

Eat some protein.

Eat some dairy.

Eat lots of fruit and vegetables.

Eat lots of carbohydrate.

1 Draw and label your favourite fruit and vegetables.

My favourite fruit and vegetables

2 Think about it!

Is there a food group you need to eat more of or less of?

CHECK YOUR LEARNING

◯ I can say which foods are healthy.

2.3 An unhealthy diet

exercise, heart, teeth

KEY FACTS

Too much fat is bad for your heart, but **exercise** can keep your **heart** strong.

Too much sugar can damage your **teeth**, but brushing your teeth can help to keep them clean and strong.

Good and bad

1 Draw things inside shapes A and B that are good for your heart and good for your teeth.

A

B

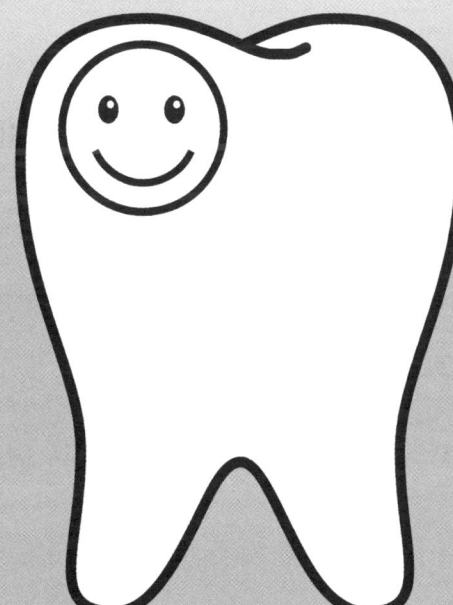

2 Looking after ourselves

2 Draw things inside shapes C and D that are **bad** for your heart and bad for your teeth.

C   D

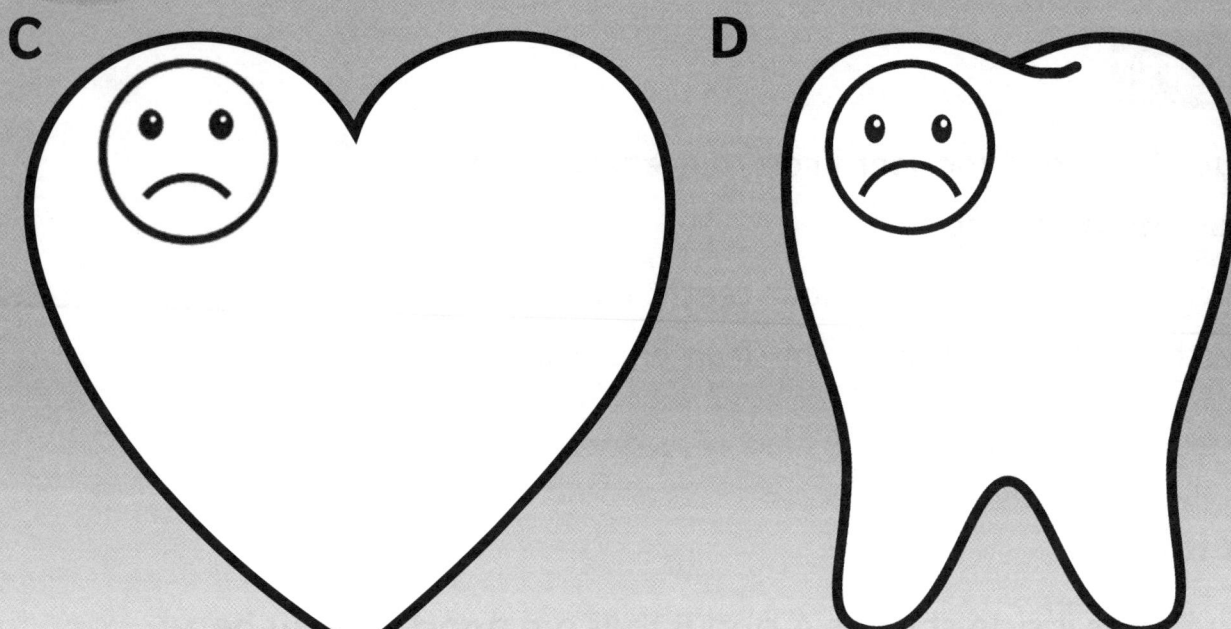

3 Think about it!

What can you do to keep healthy?

_____
_____

CHECK YOUR LEARNING

◯ I can say why fat and sugar are unhealthy.

2.4 Exercise and sleep

muscles, record

KEY FACTS

Exercise is good for your **muscles** and your heart.

Resources

You will need a clock, watch or timer to time each activity.

Testing your heart

Put your hand over your heart and close your eyes.
Can you feel your heart beating?

Remember:

Remember to shut your eyes. This will help you to focus on your heart beating.

1. Predict which of the activities in the table on the next page will make your heart beat faster, slower or the same. **Record** your predictions in the table.

2. Now do each activity for one minute. Then stop and feel your heart beating again. Record your results in the table.

3. Choose two more activities and repeat.

Activity	Prediction: Will your heart beat faster, slower or the same?	Result: Did your heart beat faster, slower or the same?
Running		
Reading a book		
Star jumps		

4 Which of the activities is not good exercise?

_____

5 Think about it!
What kind of exercise do you like best?

_____

CHECK YOUR LEARNING

 I can say why exercise is good for me.

2.4 Exercise and sleep

3 Living things

What learners will practise and reinforce

The activities in this Skills Builder unit give learners further practice in the following topics in the Learner's Book and Activity Book:

Topic	In this topic, learners will:
3.1 Living and non-living things	learn to identify the seven needs of living things
3.2 Growth and nutrition	see that plants get food from sunlight and animals get food from plants and other animals
3.3 Movement and reproduction	compare the ways different animals move learn that all living things reproduce
3.4 Sorting humans	understand that people are similar in some ways but different in others see that we can group people in different ways
3.5 Sorting living things	sort living things into groups

Help your learner

In this unit, learners will observe and compare objects and living things (Section 3.1), record observations (Section 3.3) and present results (Sections 3.4 and 3.5). They will also begin to use scientific knowledge to suggest explanations (Section 3.3). To help them:

1 Give learners opportunities to make predictions. What do they think will happen? Don't worry if these predictions are wrong; predicting is an important science skill.

TEACHING TIP

Learners need to experience familiar things, including familiar animals and plants, before they are introduced to more unusual examples.

3.1 Living and non-living

life processes, oxygen, living, non-living, observe

LOOK AND LEARN

Everything that is alive does these seven **life processes**:
- uses **oxygen**
- has senses
- can produce young
- needs food and water
- moves
- grows
- produces waste products

Living or non-living?

Look at the pictures. Are these things **living** or **non-living**? Draw a line to the right word.

living

| rose | river | spider | watch | penguin | cactus |

non-living

KEY FACTS

A car can move but it is non-living.

3.1 Living and non-living

It's alive!

1 **Observe** things outside.

Fill in the table. Two examples have been started, but you must decide if they are living or non-living.

I observed a …	Needs oxygen	Needs food and water	Can move	Has senses	Can make young	Grows	Makes waste products	Living or non-living?
mango tree	✓	✓	✓	✓	✓	✓	✓	
bicycle	✗	✗	✓	✗	✗	✗	✗	

2 **Think about it!**

When a bird lays an egg, the egg does not move and does not eat. Is the egg living or non-living?

_____

CHECK YOUR LEARNING

◯ I can say if something is a living thing and why.

◯ I can talk about the seven life processes.

3.2 Growth and nutrition

Where does food come from?

Look at the picture. All the different animals and plants need food.

1 Plants use energy from the Sun to make their own food. Draw arrows on the picture to show the sunlight shining on the plants to give them food.

2 Some animals eat other animals. Some animals eat plants. Draw a line from each picture to the correct label.

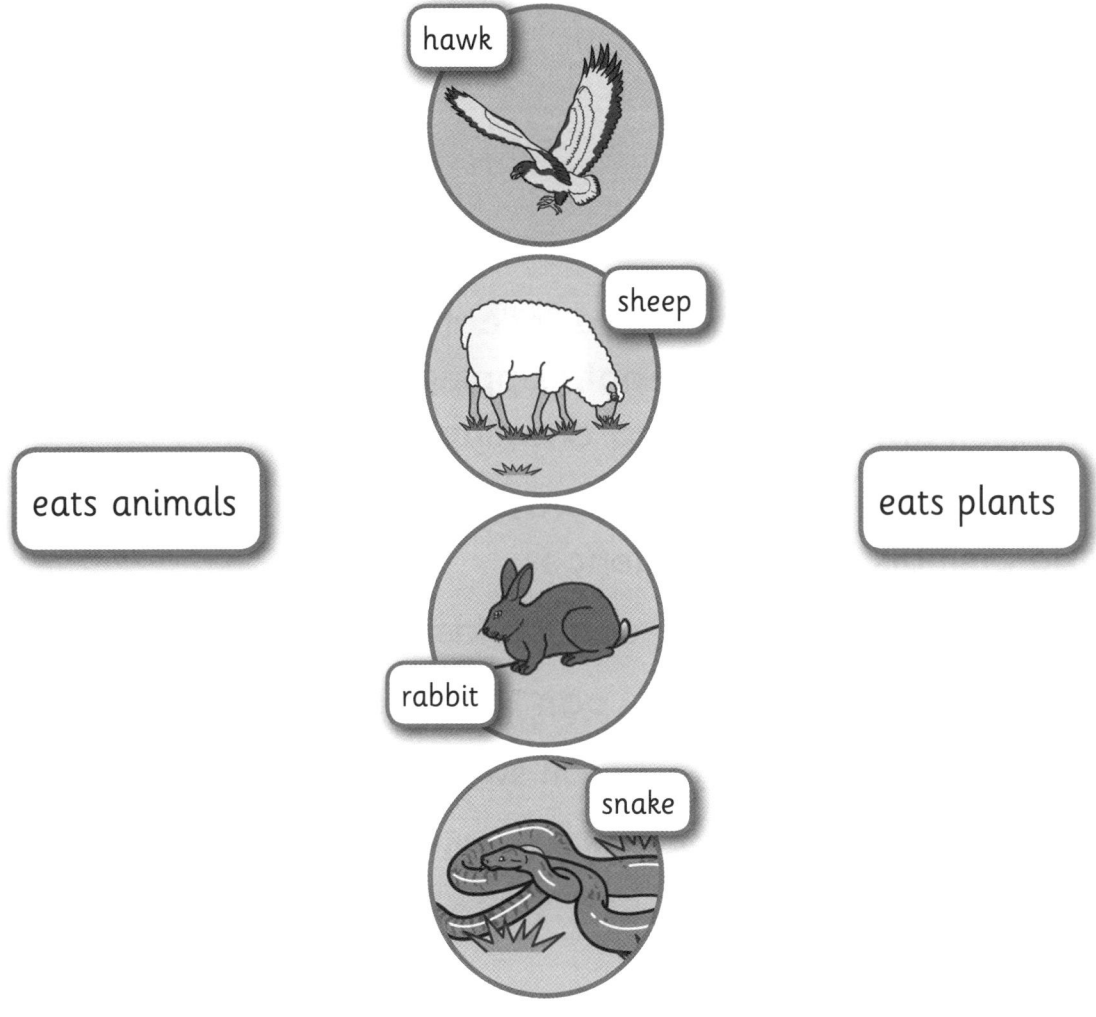

3 Think about it!

If plants use sunlight to make their food, what would happen if the Sun was not there?

_____

CHECK YOUR LEARNING

◯ I know that plants use sunlight to make food.

◯ I know that animals get food by eating plants and other animals.

3.3 Movement and reproduction

reproduce, offspring

Resources
You may want to use a skipping rope.

Ways of moving

1 Talk about the different ways you move. Try carefully bending, turning, stretching, running on the spot, skipping, moving your arms up down, left and right, blinking, crawling, rolling and so on.

2 Some animals can also move in these ways, but better or faster than you. Add animals to these sentences.

a I can run, but a _____ can run faster than me.

b I can jump, but a _____ can jump higher than me.

c I can swim, but a _____ can swim faster than me.

Some animals cannot move as well as you. Fill the gaps.

d I can run faster than a _____.

e I can jump further than a _____.

f I can walk faster than a _____.

3 Think about it!

Animals move quickly for different reasons. Why might a cheetah and an antelope have to run fast?

_____
_____

> **KEY FACTS**
>
> All living things **reproduce** (produce **offspring**).

How many babies?

1 Use the words and numbers in the box to complete the table.

> frog   yes   100   cub

Animal	Offspring	Number born or laid	Fed and cared for by parents?
whale	calf	1 or 2	yes
lion		2–4	
fish	fry	200	no
bird	chick	2–10	yes
	tadpole		no

2 Why do you think that fish and frogs do not feed and care for their babies?

_____

3 **Think about it!**

Human parents try to care for their babies for a long time. Why?

_____

CHECK YOUR LEARNING

◯ I know about different ways that living things move.

◯ I know that all living things reproduce.

3.4 Sorting humans

similar, different

Similar and different!

1 Draw two of your friends.

2 Write down the ways that you are **similar** and the ways you are **different**. For example the way you look or things that you like or don't like.

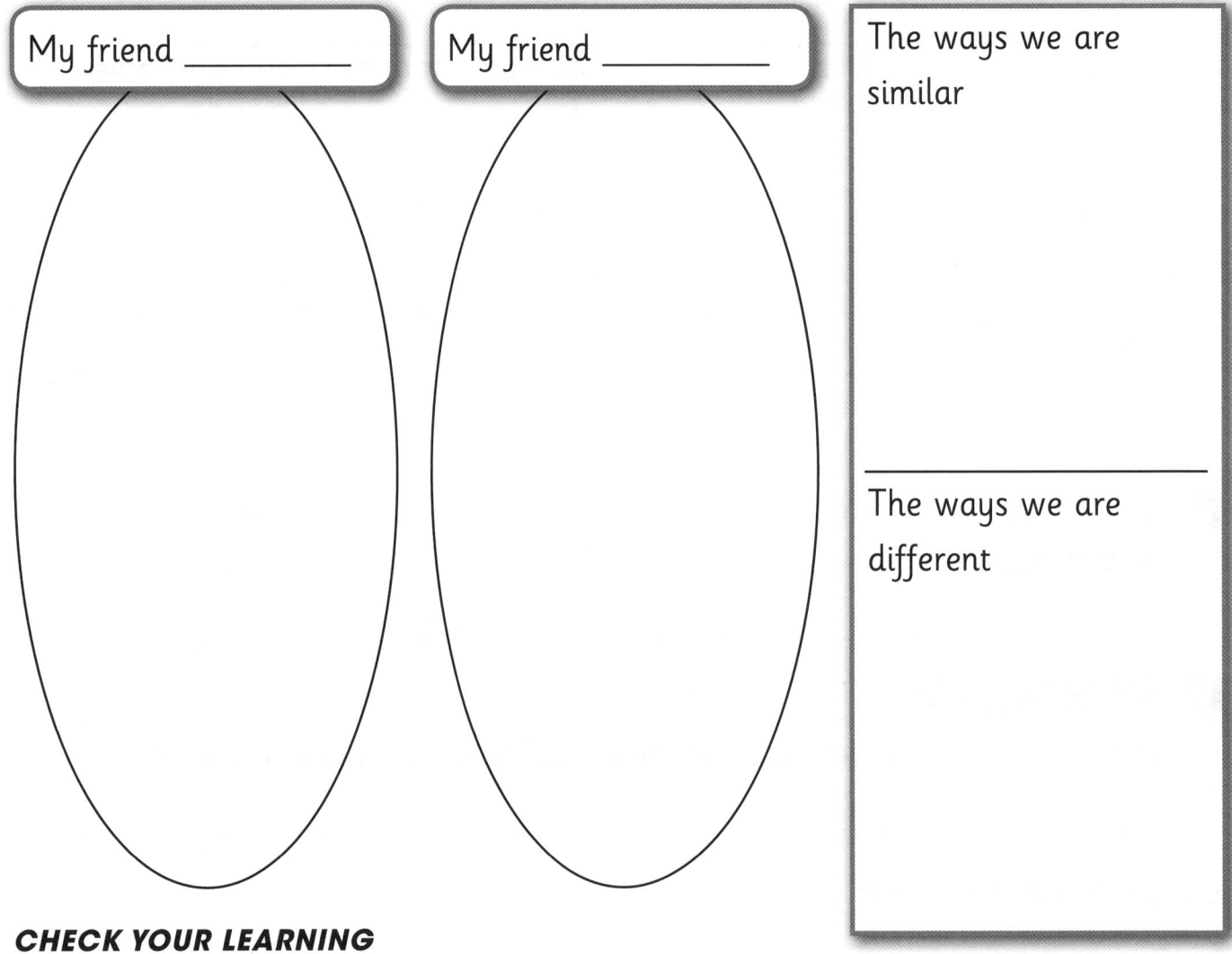

My friend _____

My friend _____

The ways we are similar

The ways we are different

CHECK YOUR LEARNING

◯ I can observe that people are similar in lots of ways.

◯ I can observe differences between people, such as hair colour and height.

3.5 Sorting living things

breathe, Venn diagram, sort

Sorting animals

Resources
You will need a big piece of paper and pens.

1 Look at the picture. Groups that we could make are: animals with legs, animals that **breathe** air, animals with claws, animals that swim.

2 Copy this **Venn diagram** on to the big piece of paper.

animals that live in the sea | animals with legs that live in the sea | animals with legs

3 Sort the animals by drawing them in the correct part of the Venn diagram.

3 Living things

Grouping plant foods we eat

Here are some foods we get from plants.

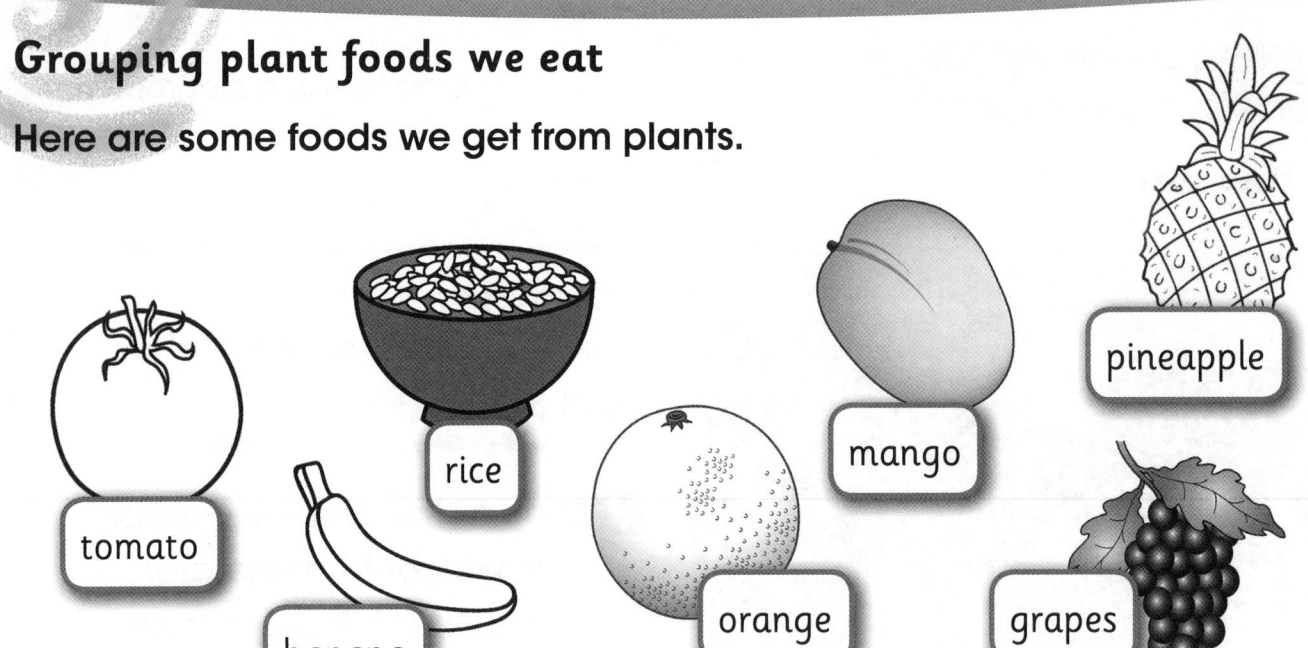

Sort the food by drawing pictures in the correct oval below.

Foods we peel to eat

Foods we don't peel to eat

KEY FACTS

Scientists have to group living things carefully so that they can study them.

CHECK YOUR LEARNING

◯ I can sort living things into groups.

◯ I observe that living things in a group have something in common.

3.5 Sorting living things

4 Our five senses

What learners will practise and reinforce

The activities in this Skills Builder unit give learners further practice in the following topics in the Learner's Book and Activity Book:

Topic	In this topic, learners will:
4.1 Hearing and touch	link each sense to the correct sense organ identify times that we use our senses
4.2 Taste and smell	test their sense of smell
4.3 Sight	learn about parts of the human eye learn about the eyesight of humans and different animals

Help your learner

In this unit, learners will practise observing and comparing objects, living things and events (Section 4.1) and collecting evidence (Section 4.2). They will also use scientific knowledge to suggest explanations (Section 4.3). To help them:

1. Encourage learners' curiosity by listening to their questions and talking about them. Don't worry if you don't know an answer: you can discover it together.

2. When learners conduct practical science investigations, encourage them to plan. Support their decisions. Making some wrong decisions is part of science – as long as they learn from them.

! Stress safety when talking about the senses. For example remind learners to never look directly at the Sun and avoid loud sounds.

TEACHING TIP

When you talk with learners about taste, try to refer to bitter and sour tastes as well as sweet. They may not be so familiar, but they are important in science.

4.1 Hearing and touch

hearing, touch, smell, taste, sight

Our five senses

Look at Anita. Draw arrows from the labels to the parts of her body that give her each sense.

Which sense would I use?

Look at each picture. Would you use the sense of hearing or touch?

I would use my sense of _____

I would use my sense of _____

I would use my sense of _____

I would use my sense of _____

I would use my sense of _____

I would use my sense of _____

CHECK YOUR LEARNING

○ I can name the five human senses.

○ I know about the sense of hearing and the sense of touch.

4.2 Taste and smell

sweet, nostrils

KEY FACTS

Our senses of smell and taste often work together. They help us to avoid eating bad food.

⚠️ Take care when smelling things in case they are dangerous. Always smell from at least 10 cm away.

Smell the food

1 Find five different safe foods. Can you smell them? Record here what you can smell.

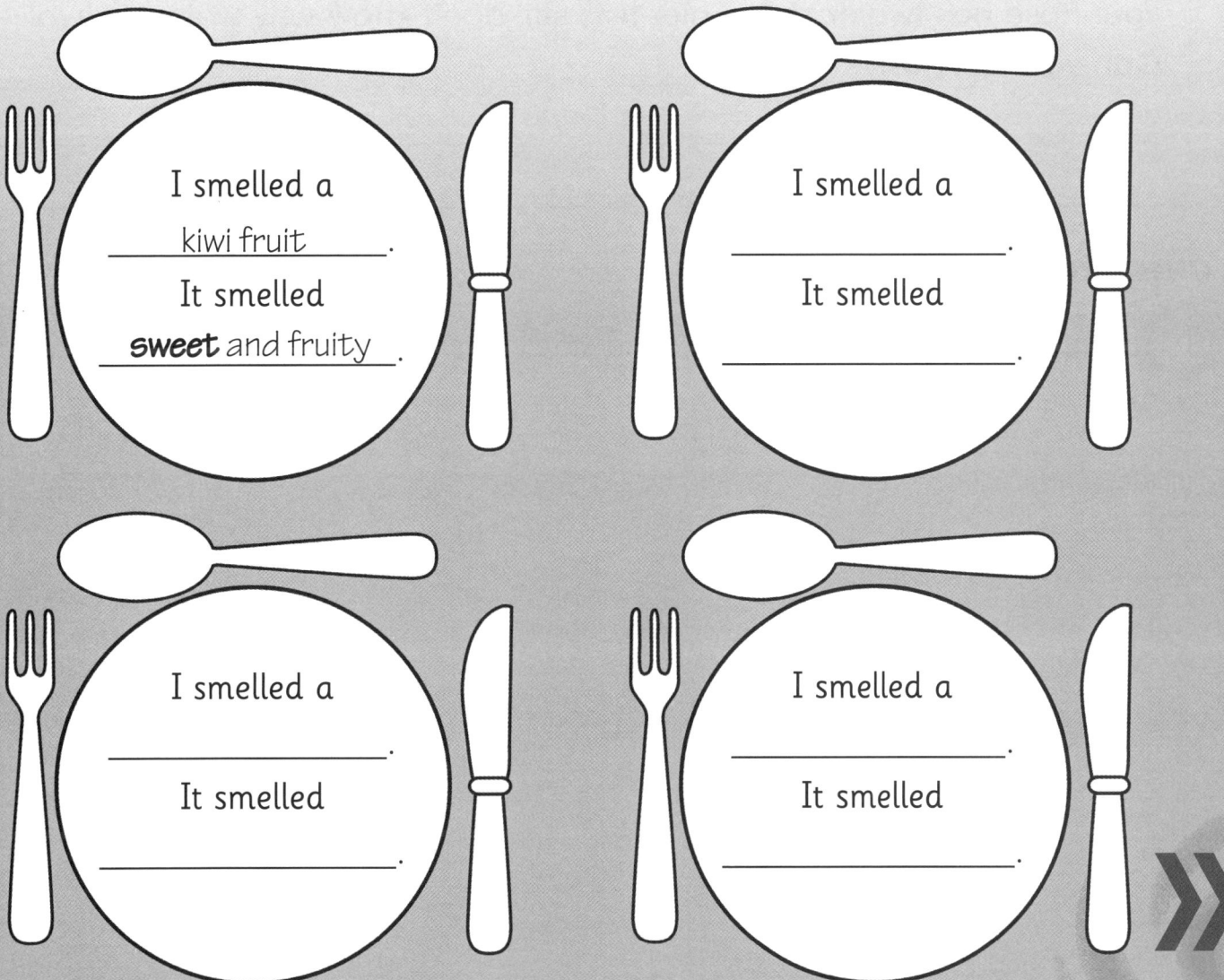

I smelled a _kiwi fruit_. It smelled **sweet** and fruity.

I smelled a _____. It smelled _____.

I smelled a _____. It smelled _____.

I smelled a _____. It smelled _____.

4 Our five senses

I smelled a _____.
It smelled _____.

I smelled a _____.
It smelled _____.

2 Think about it!

Your nose has two **nostrils**. Scientists still don't know why we have two! Can you think why?

_____

_____

CHECK YOUR LEARNING

○ I know that the senses of taste and smell often work together.

4.3 Sight

> eyelash, pupil, eyelid

Parts of the eye

Use the key words to label the picture of the eye.

⚠️ Look after your eyes. Never put things in your eye and never look at the Sun.

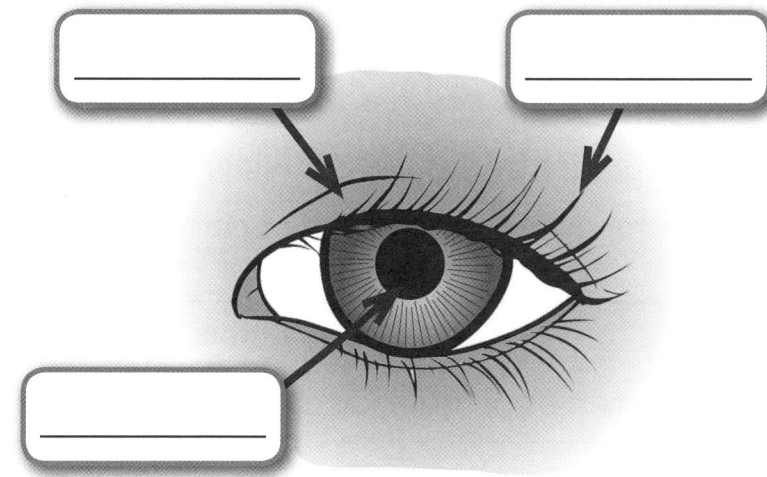

Good and poor eyesight

Choose an animal to fill each gap and answer these questions.

1 Why does a _____ need good eyesight?

_____

2 Why might a _____ have poor eyesight?

_____

 mole

 hawk

 worm

 cat

CHECK YOUR LEARNING

◯ I know that I see with my eyes.

◯ I know that some animals have good eyesight and some have poor eyesight.

5 Investigating materials

What learners will practise and reinforce

The activities in this Skills Builder unit give learners further practice in the following topics in the Learner's Book and Activity Book:

Topic	In this topic, learners will:
5.1 Properties of materials	name some different materials
5.2 Sorting materials	sort materials by strength and texture
5.3 Uses of materials	see Challenge, Section 5.3
5.4 Testing materials	see Challenge, Section 5.4
5.5 Magnetic materials	investigate whether all metal is magnetic

Help your learner

In this unit, learners will practise observing and comparing objects, living things and events (Sections 5.1 and 5.2). They will also make generalisations and begin to identify simple patterns in results (Section 5.5). To help them:

1 Ask learners to close their eyes when touching materials. This will encourage them to make more use of their sense of touch.

2 There are many names of materials to learn. Help learners to make a poster of material names or make name labels for the different materials they find at home or at school.

TEACHING TIP

Materials are usually made into objects. Encourage learners to talk about the properties of the material rather than the properties of the object.

5.1 Properties of materials

material, metal, wood, paper, plastic, glass

Name the material

1 Find each object in the table below.

2 Name the **material** it is made from. Use the key words to help you.

Object	Find it	Material
(coin)	✔ I found it!	metal
(felt tip pen)	☐ I found it!	
(window)	☐ I found it!	
(newspaper)	☐ I found it!	
(branch)	☐ I found it!	
(door handle)	☐ I found it!	

3 Think about it!

Which of these materials does not have to be made?

_____

CHECK YOUR LEARNING

○ I can name some materials.

5 Investigating materials

5.2 Sorting materials

property, weak, strong, rough, smooth, flexible, rigid

LOOK AND LEARN

Materials have **properties**. They can be **weak** or **strong**. They can be **rough** or **smooth**. Materials are chosen carefully for their properties to make different things. For example a chair can be made of wood that is strong enough for people to sit on.

Materials and properties

Which material is weak and which is strong?

weak

strong

Which material is rough and which is smooth?

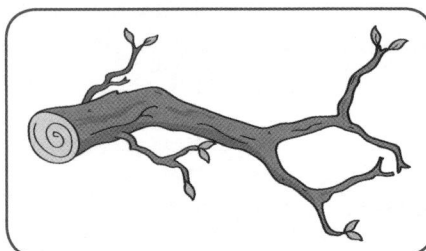

rough

smooth

38 5.2 Sorting materials

Sorting materials by testing

1 Find some objects made from a single material.

2 Test them to see if they are easy to bend.

3 If they are easy to bend, draw them in the **flexible** group.

4 If they are hard to bend, draw them in the **rigid** group.

5 Write the material they are made from.

Flexible	Rigid
cotton	stone

6 Think about it!

Why does a coin need to be strong?

_____

_____

CHECK YOUR LEARNING

○ I can sort materials by their properties.

○ I know that materials are chosen for different jobs because of their properties.

5 Investigating materials 39

5.5 Magnetic materials

magnet, magnetic, non-magnetic

Testing metal

Resources
You will need a **magnet**.

1 Find three different coins and three other objects made from metal.

2 Use a magnet to find out if the metals are **magnetic** or **non-magnetic**.

3 Draw and label the objects in the results table.

Magnetic	Non-magnetic
paper clip	

4 Are all metals magnetic?

_____

5 Think about it!

Are any other materials magnetic?

_____

CHECK YOUR LEARNING

○ I know that only some materials are magnetic.

6 Forces and movement

What learners will practise and reinforce

The activities in this Skills Builder unit give learners further practice in the following topics in the Learner's Book and Activity Book:

Topic	In this topic, learners will:
6.1 Push and pull	explore the forces of push and pull in everyday life
6.2 Changing shape	use forces to change the shape of things
6.3 How big is that force?	identify different sizes of forces
6.4 Forcemeters	measure forces using elastic
6.5 Friction	learn that friction is a force made by two surfaces rubbing together

Help your learner

In this unit, learners will practise observing and comparing objects, living things and events (Section 6.1), making predictions and collecting evidence (Section 6.5). They will also record observations (Section 6.4), present results and begin to use scientific knowledge to suggest explanations (Section 6.5). To help them:

1 Encourage learners to ask questions about forces and talk about forces in action, for example when they are pushing a toy or playing on a seesaw or swing.

2 Look for ways to allow learners to feel forces and to see them manifested in elastic materials stretching, for example blowing up a balloon.

TEACHING TIP

Give learners lots of opportunities to talk about pushes and pulls they encounter as well as opportunities to ask questions and carry out investigations.

6.1 Push and pull

force, push, pull

KEY FACTS

Forces are all around us. **Push** and **pull** are both forces.

Push-pull explorer

1 How many pushes and pulls can you find in the room?

Write them in the table below.

Things that I pushed	Things that I pulled
	I pulled the curtains closed.

2 Which thing you tested needed the biggest push?
_____

3 Which thing you tested needed the biggest pull?
_____

Take care when pushing and pulling. Don't put yourself or another person in danger.

Push and pull sports

1 Look at these sports and decide if the player has to pull or push. Draw an arrow on the picture to show the push or pull.

2 What is your favourite game? Do you have to push or pull?

_____

3 **Think about it!**

Some weightlifters can pull and lift a car. If you were this strong, what would you do to help other people?

_____

CHECK YOUR LEARNING

○ I know that pulls and pushes are forces.

○ I can talk about forces we use in sports and everyday.

6.2 Changing shape

elastic

Shaping materials

> **Resources**
> You will need modelling material (such as clay), card, metal foil, **elastic**, a biscuit and a piece of rock.

1 Test each material to see if you can change its shape by pushing or pulling the material.

Test number _____	Test number _____	Test number _____
Material _____	Material _____	Material _____
Change shape by:	Change shape by:	Change shape by:
☐ pushing?	☐ pushing?	☐ pushing?
☐ pulling?	☐ pulling?	☐ pulling?

Test number _____	Test number _____	Test number _____
Material _____	Material _____	Material _____
Change shape by:	Change shape by:	Change shape by:
☐ pushing?	☐ pushing?	☐ pushing?
☐ pulling?	☐ pulling?	☐ pulling?

2 Now complete this sentence.

I could change the shape of some materials when I _____ and _____ because these materials were _____.

> **Remember:**
> Sometimes we need materials to be flexible. Sometimes we need materials that are very strong and rigid, for example when we build houses and bridges.

Modelling wet sand

Resources
You will need wet sand and a spoon or stick.

Have you ever made models in the sand on a beach or by a river? You model the sand using forces.

1 Make three drawings below and use arrows and words to show that you use forces to shape the sand to make your model. Use these words to help you.

dig   push   pull
press   pat   smooth

First I will ...	Then I will ...	After this I will ...

2 Think about it!
How many workers can you name who have to shape materials in their job?

_____

_____

_____

CHECK YOUR LEARNING

○ I know that we can use forces to change the shape of materials.

○ I know that some materials can be shaped by hand but others cannot.

6 Forces and movement   **45**

6.3 How big is that force?

What a big push!

Some pushes are very small and some are huge! Draw a line from each bulldozer to the right words to describe the force.

a small push

a big pull

a large push

a very large push

a small pull

a very small push

KEY FACTS

When a rocket takes off, the engine has to push up very hard to lift the rocket.

CHECK YOUR LEARNING

○ I know that there are different sizes of forces.

6.4 Forcemeters

forcemeter, measure, newton

Elastic shows us the force

LOOK AND LEARN

A **forcemeter** is any device that shows us the size of a force. An elastic band can work as a pull forcemeter.

Resources
You will need a ruler, string, scissors, a paper clip, a strong elastic band and objects to pull (for example a book, a stone, a feather, a pencil case and so on).

! Take care with elastic bands and when you pull things.

1. On a table arrange six objects you can pull. You might like to tie string around some. Put a paper clip onto an elastic band so that you can easily attach it to objects.

2. Hold one end of the elastic band and attach the other to an object. Slowly pull on the elastic until the object moves. Observe what happens to the elastic band. Use a ruler to **measure** the length of the elastic band when the object starts to move.

6 Forces and movement

47

Record your results here.

Object	Measurement
A book	The elastic stretched to _____ cm.
	The elastic stretched to _____ cm.
	The elastic stretched to _____ cm.
	The elastic stretched to _____ cm.
	The elastic stretched to _____ cm.
	The elastic stretched to _____ cm.

3 Which object required the most force?

_____

4 Which was the easiest to move?

_____

Newton meter measures forces

In this activity, you measure and record results.

> **KEY FACTS**
>
> A Newton meter is a special forcemeter used by scientists. It measures a force in **newtons** (N).

Look at the Newton meters – each is pulling a type of footwear. Read each Newton meter and write the results in the table in order from the biggest force to the smallest force.

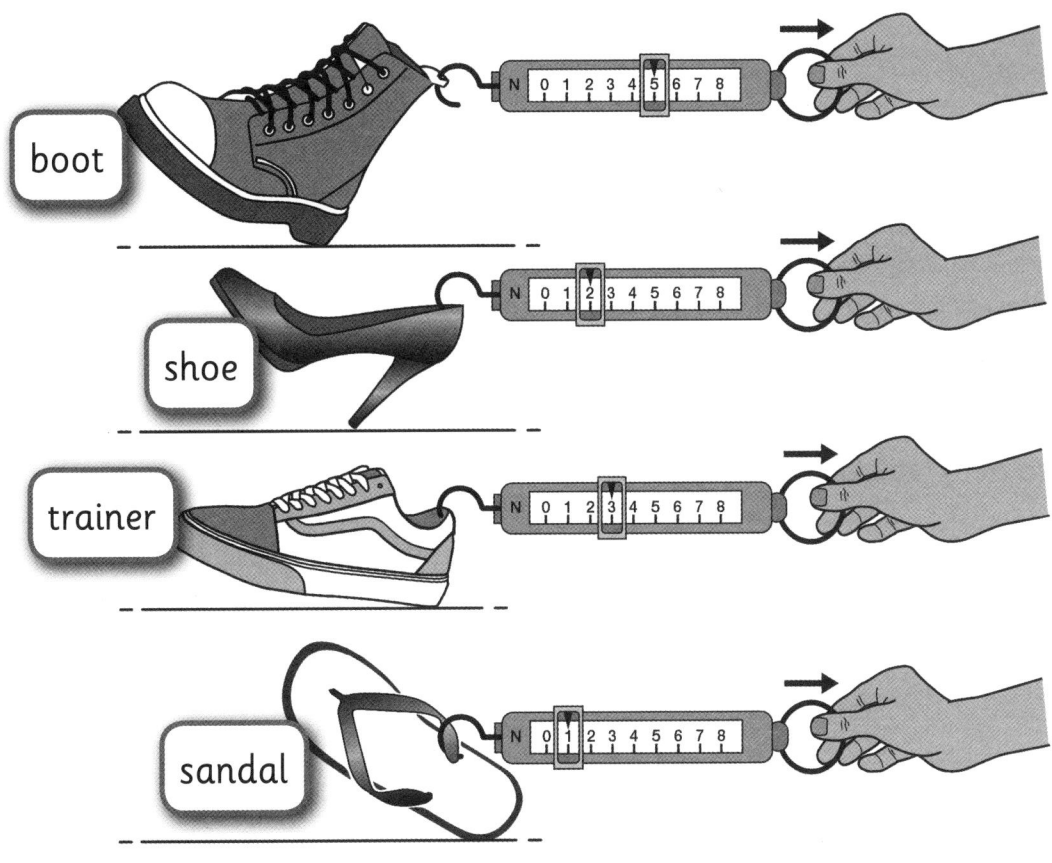

Type of footwear	Force needed to pull it

CHECK YOUR LEARNING

◯ I know that forces can be measured with a forcemeter.

6.5 Friction

friction, surface, grip, gravity

LOOK AND LEARN

Friction is a force made when two **surfaces** rub together. Smooth surfaces make less friction. Rough surfaces **grip** one another and make more friction.

Is the coin sticky?

Resources
You will need a coin and two rulers.

1. Place one ruler flat on the table. Place the coin on the ruler in the middle. Raise one end of the ruler by 1 cm. Does the coin move?
   _____

2. Raise the end of the ruler up to 5 cm. You now have a steeper slope. Does the coin move? _____

3. Complete the sentence.

   The coin does not move because the force of _____ is holding it.

4. How many centimetres high do you have to lift the ruler to make the coin move? _____

5. What force makes the coin move down? _____

> **KEY FACTS**
>
> Forces can make things change direction.

Think about it!

6 Climbers have to climb steep mountain slopes covered in ice. What can they do to stop themselves from sliding down?

_____

_____

7 What force might make a climber change direction and slide down?

_____

> **Remember:**
>
> Friction can help us when we want to walk across a surface. Friction can also hurt us when we fall.

CHECK YOUR LEARNING

◯ I know that friction is a force.

◯ I know that friction is caused by surfaces rubbing together.

◯ I know that the size of the friction force depends on the surfaces that are rubbing together.

◯ I know forces can make things change direction.

Answers

1 Looking after plants

1.1

Plant parts

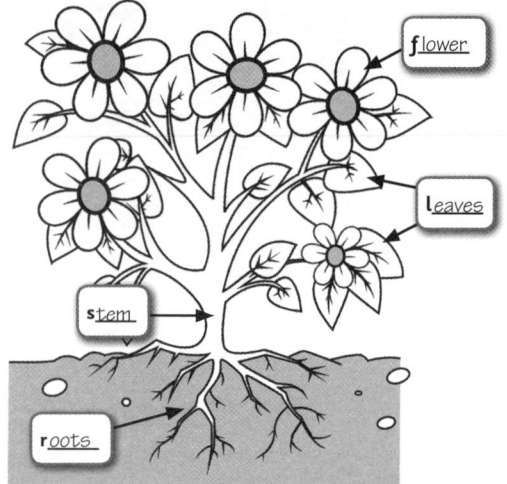

Label a real plant

The learner should have added labels to a real plant as shown in the picture in the main part of the book.

1.2

Plant height

1. Plant 1 8 cm. Plant 2 4 cm. Plant 3 10 cm. Plant 4 4 cm.
2. light
3. water and light
4. **Think about it!**
   Outdoor plants get water from rain that soaks into the soil.

1.3

No roots!

Think about it!

7. Plants need healthy roots and stems to transport water.
8. The plant with no roots died because it could not get enough water. Without roots, the plant cannot absorb water from the soil.

1.4

What is the temperature?

1.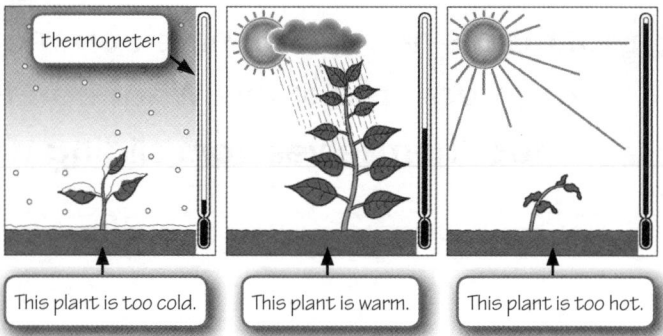

2. **Think about it!**
   Plant 3 needs to be in a warm place, not a hot place. It also needs water.

2 Looking after ourselves

2.1

Which food, which group?

Food hunt

1 and 2 Answers will depend on the food chosen. Use the food triangle in Section 2.2 to check them.

3. **Think about it!**
   The learner should have identified fat and sugar as the most unhealthy food group.

2.2

Healthy food I love

1 Pictures of fruit and vegetables only

2 Think about it!
Answers will depend on the learner's own diet.

2.3

Good and bad

1 The learner's own drawings to show:
A exercise
B toothbrush or brushing of teeth

2 The learner's own drawings to show:
C cake or other food from the fat and sugar group
D sweets or other very sweet food

3 Think about it!
To keep healthy, do exercise, brush your teeth and eat lots of fruit and vegetables.

2.4

Testing your heart

1 The learner should have recorded their predictions in the table.

2 Running – heart beats faster
Reading a book – heart beats slower or the same
Star jumps – heart beats faster

4 Reading a book is not good exercise.

5 Think about it!
This will be a personal response, but any activity that makes the heart beat faster is good exercise.

3 Living things

3.1

Living or non-living?

1 The pictures should be linked to labels as follows:
rose – living
river – non-living
spider – living
watch – non-living
penguin – living
cactus – living

It's alive!

1 The learner should respond in a consistent way so that only things which have all the characteristics of living things are identified as living. They should have recognised that the mango tree is living and the bicycle is non-living.

2 Think about it!
Most eggs of birds in the wild have within them a living thing. The eggshell itself is not living but the tiny baby bird inside is alive. Be aware that the eggs bought in shops are usually infertile and don't contain a live baby bird.

3.2

Where does food come from?

1 The learner should have drawn arrows from the Sun down to the plants.

2 The learner should have drawn lines from hawk and snake to eats animals and lines from rabbit and sheep to eats plants.

3 Think about it!
If the Sun was not there, it would be very cold. The plants would all die and so would the animals that eat plants and then the animals that eat animals.

3.3

Ways of moving

1 The learner should talk about the many ways that humans can move.

2 Many responses are possible:
a For example tiger, cheetah, antelope, wolf.
b For example kangaroo, dolphin.
c For example tuna, shark, eel.
d For example snail, hamster, worm.
e For example spider, ant, hamster.
f For example slug, tortoise.

3 Think about it!
Some animals move quickly to catch and eat other animals. Other animals move quickly so that they will not be caught and eaten.

How many babies?

1 The learner should have filled in these rows as follows:

| lion | cub | 2–4 | yes |
| frog | tadpole | 100 | no |

2 Fish and frogs produce many babies in the water and so the babies are soon swept away and cannot be fed and cared for.

3 Think about it!
Humans look after their young for a long time because they try to make sure each child is safe and grows to be an adult.

3.4
Similar and different!

1 The learner will have drawn two friends.

2 A list of similarities such as: we both have hair, clothes, freckles, toys, parents, brothers and sisters, a pet. We both like TV, games, music, computers. A list of differences such as: eye colour, hair colour, freckles, handedness, height, mass, likes and dislikes for example colours, food and so on.

3.5
Sorting animals

3 Venn diagram with two overlapping circles making three sectors:
animals that live in the sea – seal, whale, dolphin, jellyfish, fish, sea snake, sea slug
animals with legs – human boy and girl, gull
intersection – crab, octopus, lobster

Grouping plant foods we eat

Foods we peel to eat: banana, orange, mango, pineapple
Foods we don't peel to eat: grapes, rice, tomato

4 Our five senses
4.1
Our five senses

Lines are drawn from the labels: sight to eye or eyes, hearing to an ear or ears, smell to the nose or nostril, taste to the tongue, touch to any part of the skin.

Which sense would I use?

The learner should have filled in the gaps as follows: bell – hearing, warm cup – touch, bird – hearing, radio – hearing, mobile phone – hearing, prickly leaf – touch.

4.2
Smell the food

1 The learner should have described the smell of five foods. You can accept any answers that refer to smells.

2 Think about it!
Accept any reasoned answer, for example so that if one nostril is hurt, we have a spare. Or so we can smell to the left and right or so we can smell things better.

4.3
Parts of the eye

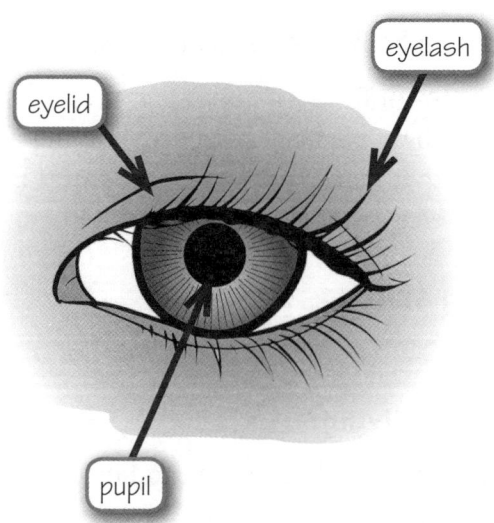

Good and poor eyesight

1 The learner should have chosen an animal with good eyesight (for example hawk or cat) and explained this need in terms of hunting for food or seeing danger.

2 The learner should have chosen an animal with poor eyesight (for example worm or mole) and explained this need in terms of living in the dark and/or using other senses.

5 Investigating materials

5.1

Name the material

1 and **2** The learner should have found objects like the ones in the table and named the materials as follows: pen – plastic, window – glass (or glass and wood/plastic), newspaper – paper, stick – wood, door handle – metal.

3 *Think about it!*
Wood does not have to be made. Wood comes from the trunks of trees.

5.2

Materials and properties

The learner should have drawn a line from the coin to strong, the newspaper to weak, the twig to rough, the window to smooth.

Sorting materials by testing

1 to **5** Answers depend on the objects used.

6 *Think about it!*
A coin needs to be strong because many different people use it for a long time. If it was weak, it would get damaged.

5.5

Testing metal

1 to **3** Answers depend on the objects tested.

4 Not all metals are magnetic.

5 *Think about it!*
No other common materials are magnetic. (There are some naturally magnetic types of stone but they are very rare.)

6 Forces and movement

6.1

Push-pull explorer

1 The learner should have completed the table with examples like these:

Things that I pushed	Things that I pulled
I pushed to close the door.	I pulled the blind down.
I pushed a chair.	I pulled the rug on the floor.
I pushed a drawer shut.	I pulled a bag open.
I pushed a plant on the table.	I pulled sticky tape off the roll.
I pushed a plate.	I pulled my shoelaces tight.

2 They should identify a big push based on their observations.

3 They should identify a big pull based on their observations.

Push and pull sports

1 Pictures should include these features (it is most important that the word push or pull is used):
Kicking a ball – push the ball with the foot. An arrow from the foot to the ball.
Tug of war – either an arrow pushing the feet on the floor or an opposite arrow showing the hands pulling on the rope.
Tennis – push the ball with the racket. An arrow from the racket to the ball.
Weightlifting – pull the bar up. An arrow from the hands pointing upwards.

2 Personal answer

3 *Think about it!*
The learner should talk about good things they could do if they were very strong, for example helping others lift things, doing jobs and work, rescuing animals and people.

6.2

Shaping materials

1 The learner should have tested six materials and for each recorded a test number, the name of the materials and whether they changed its shape by pulling or pushing.

2 For example:

I could change the shape of some materials when I pushed and pulled because these materials were flexible. Alternatives to flexible include weak, bendy, soft and so on.

Modelling wet sand

1 The learner will have drawn three stages in the construction of their shape. They should have drawn arrows to show the way the sand is pushed or pulled. There should be writing to indicate what is happening in the pictures. The writing should talk about shaping the sand by pushing and pulling sand. They may use other words such as pat, press, dig, smooth.

2 *Think about it!*

The learner might suggest a number of occupations that require the use of forces to shape materials, for example farmer, builder, sculptor, carpenter, plumber, tree cutter, boat builder, stonemason, artist, potter, baker, cook and so on.

6.3

What a big push!

The bulldozer pushing the sack should be linked to a small push or a very small push. The bulldozer pushing the pile of soil should be linked to a large push. The bulldozer pushing the large pile of rocks should be linked to a very large push.

6.4

Elastic shows us the force

2 For each object, the learner should have recorded the stretch of the elastic band in centimetres.

3 The learner should have identified which object needed the greatest force.

4 The learner should have identified which object needed the least force.

Newton meter measures force

The learner should have recorded these results in this order (from the biggest to the smallest force):

boot = 5N
trainer = 3N
shoe = 2N
sandal = 1N

6.5

Is the coin sticky?

1 no

2 probably no

3 friction

4 The learner should give the result in cm. They should explain the friction is not holding it now. They may refer to gravity pulling.

5 gravity

Think about it!

6 Climbers stop themselves falling by using more friction, for example holding onto a rope, using an ice axe or using crampons or spikes on their boots.

7 gravity

Glossary

> **Remember:** Practise saying these words aloud. Try to use them when talking about the topic.

1 Looking after plants

absorb	to soak up liquid
cold	a temperature which is low
flowers	part of the plant where seeds are made
grow	to become larger and more developed
height	how tall something is
hot	a temperature which is high
investigation	a test or experiment to find something out
leaves	part of the plant where the plant's food is produced
light	energy that comes from the Sun or a light bulb
plant	a living thing that grows and has roots, a stem, leaves and often flowers
predict	to think carefully about what might happen
question	a sentence that states what you would like to find out
results	the observations or measurements made in a test
roots	parts of a plant that support the plant and collect water from the soil
soil	the natural material on the surface of the Earth in which plants grow
stem	part of the plant that transports water around the plant
temperature	how hot or cold something is
thermometer	an object used to measure temperature
transport	to move something
warm	a temperature between hot and cold
water	a clear liquid that all living things need to survive

2 Looking after ourselves

carbohydrate	food that gives your body energy
dairy	foods that have milk in them
diet	the foods that you eat
exercise	moving around so that your heart beats faster
fat and sugar	you need a little fat and sugar but too much is bad for your body
food group	foods are grouped by what they do to the body
fruit and vegetables	fruit and vegetables keep your body healthy
healthy	good for your body
heart	your heart pumps blood around your body
muscles	your muscles can make your body move
protein	food that your body uses for growth and repair, for example meat and fish
record	to write or draw results to show what happened
teeth	you use your teeth to chew food in your mouth
unhealthy	bad for your body

3 Living things

breathe	to take air in and out of your lungs
different	not the same
life processes	things that all living things do
living	alive
non-living	not alive
observe	to look closely to find things out
offspring	the young of an animal
oxygen	a gas found in the air that people need to breathe to live
reproduce	the life process of having babies, laying eggs or producing seeds

Remember:

Practise saying these words aloud. Try to use them when talking about the topic.

similar	when things are the same in some ways but not exactly the same
sort	to put things into groups
Venn diagram	a way of sorting data using overlapping circles

4 Our five senses

eyelash	rows of hairs on your eyelid that sense objects too close to your eye
eyelid	flap of skin that protects your eye
hearing	the sense that uses your ears to hear
nostrils	two holes in the nose that you use to smell and breathe air in
pupil	black centre of your eye, through which light enters the eye
sight	the sense that uses your eyes to see
smell	the sense that uses your nose to smell
sweet	the taste of sugar or honey
taste	the sense that uses your tongue to taste
touch	the sense that uses your skin to feel

5 Investigating materials

flexible	can be bent
glass	a material that is see-through but can be easily broken; glass is made from sand
magnet	an object that attracts magnetic materials
magnetic	a material that is attracted to a magnet
material	the thing that an object is made from, for example windows are made from a material called glass
metal	a material that is often grey, shiny and very strong
non-magnetic	a material that is not attracted to a magnet
paper	a thin, flexible material that we write on and make books from

plastic	a material that is strong and light and can be easily coloured and made into different shapes
property	what something is like, for example a mirror is smooth and shiny
rigid	a rigid object keeps its shape, is not easy to bend or stretch, is not flexible
rough	feels bumpy to the touch
smooth	something that is flat, not bumpy
strong	hard to break or damage
weak	easy to break or damage
wood	a material that comes from the trunk of a tree

6 Forces and movement

elastic	a material that can stretch but then returns to its original shape
force	a push, a pull or a twist
forcemeter	something used to measure force
friction	the force between two objects when they rub together
gravity	a force that pulls everything down to the ground
grip	to hold on to a surface
measure	to find the size or amount of something, for example length or time
newton (N)	the unit of force – force is measured in newtons
pull	to use a force to move something towards you
push	to use a force to move something away from you
surface	the outside part or top layer of something

Remember:

Practise saying these words aloud. Try to use them when talking about the topic.